SITE ACQUISITION

BRIAN YOUNG

Cover image

Remission, by Cameron Martin
Acrylic on canvas, 2006
80 x 132 inches (203.2 x 335.3 cm)
Courtesy the artist &
Greenberg Van Doren Gallery, NY

Book design by

Rebecca Wolff

Published in the United States by

Fence Books
Science Library 320
University at Albany
1400 Washington Avenue
Albany, NY 12222
www.fenceportal.org

Fence Books are distributed by

University Press of New England
www.upne.com

and printed in Canada by

Westcan Printing Group
www.westcanpg.com

Library of Congress Cataloguing in Publication Data
        Young, Brian [1959–]
        Site Acquisition/ Brian Young

Library of Congress Control Number: 2008934251

ISBN 1-934200-15-8
ISBN 13: 978-1-934200-15-5

FIRST EDITION

Some of these poems have appeared in the following magazines, to whose editors grateful acknowledgment is made: *Bayou, Colorado Review, Court Green, Denver Quarterly, Fence, Interim, Pool,* and *Volt.*

FENCE BOOKS are published in partnership with the University at Albany and the New York State Writers Institute, and with help from the New York State Council on the Arts and the National Endowment for the Arts.

SITE ACQUISITION

BRIAN YOUNG

FENCE BOOKS

ALBANY, NEW YORK

CONTENTS

[   ]   1
Save As   3
Flash Map   4
Intersection   5
Originating Without a Weapon   6
An Altar out of the Field   7
Swill   9
Down by the Tower   10
Eating Quinoa and Spelt   11
A Lush   12
Day Sleeper   13
524 E. 11th #9   15
Collecting Evidence   16
Fear of Novelty   18
The Crackheads   19
Latch/Thatch   22
The Present   23
Blurb   24
Stilt 1   25
Stilt 2   27
Stilt 3   29
Stilt 4   30
Stilt 5   31
Stilt 6   32
Stilt 69   33
Stilt 7   34
Stilt 8   35
Stilt 8 ½   37
Revolution #9   38
Stilt 9   40
Stilt 10   41
Stilt 11   42
Stilt 12   43
New to the Area   44
Charges   45
Getting Chainy   46

Backwards   47
Dead Horse Point   48
Before Daybreak   49
Hotel Halliburton   50
Frozen Emblem   51
26 Lines   52
It Already Knows You   53
Plagiarize It   55
The Sealing Eye   56
Numen Anaesthetized   58
The Long Way Around   60
Leaving   63
Always Always Land   64

For Jenny

[

From the Deseret Lounge
it is two blocks
to the Bel Air
Bar X is another
two blocks beyond
that it's easy

though the getting
back can be,
at times, more
challenging

you call
it sauce it
calls you
creature

]

SAVE AS

That is going to
  Fall over. Once it has,
  Again, been left
Running "down there."

But is altogether
Missing now, outside of the
"Backdrop." That it is
Going to give itself

  A name, only to lose
  One, so that the nameless

Dog is scratching
Its back against
This dry grass. The sun,
Then, in a brief

Case blown open,
Appears. But who is
Here to have it,
To bang for? That is,

  Going to fall.

FLASH MAP

To get scattered
About, that's natural enough, that may even
Be what it's all about.
                              Not to be
Sealed up,
                    Inside a defining concept
                              Or an enigmatic acknowledgment
Page, pager, choir boy
                    Getting screwed inside
                              The perimeter   Whispering
Persimmon   To J: At Almond Butter Falls   The personal
Affront   All being now
                    So tight-assed   Extremely vile and conformist
          The violets assaulted
                    The lamb roasting in the park
The shakes   A public dereliction
                              That has become so dreary

How to cut these lines evenly?
Now it must be
                    Coiled behind, or inside, the sun
                              Your precious trash
                                   Of precision   And damned-up
Visage in the glam   The sunken trough
          Of the damned   In the spa-like curves
                                   Of their dreams   And the lure
Of the expansive green
                    Towers Over the artificial pond
Where the frog drops in —Plop—
The country drains out
                    Its memory banks   Leaving the garden
Too lovely to enter   Out of love
As we are now
          In the Earth's long shadows   The last patches
Of melting snow

INTERSECTION

Naturally, it took over, taking all
To an unforgiving correction, that psalm
In which nothing floats, even the eye
That has tried and tried to give back
A bloodless dawn. If it was able

To open, it would upon a psychosis
That takes to the field, sends out
A secondary impulse both measured
And sequential. It would put the lens
Into the pill, upon the pulse.

Everyone was already waiting
Wirelessly anyway. Just sign
The lease, okay? Then you will go
To sleep for days, in colored rocks,
And awake as someone else entirely,
With cool, clear water flowing by.

ORIGINATING WITHOUT A WEAPON

I felt too clearly delineated, fictive
Prior to this partying with Finlandia
In the early morning, painted upon,
The sky unmoving, unremoved,
As though it was in its screen-saver mode,

And the page covered in snow
Swept me off
The plastering
Into a calculation of posture,
Out to the narcoleptic pasture,

And later in the bus transfer itself, later in
The lame monologue of ideological illusion,
I felt the maliciousness of tendency towards
The cherished zeitgeist as it chews us up.

It's been so long since I've dragged myself out
And over to the Kimchi Museum between Belle Plaine and Grace

That glint upon what was new

It may be that it found a waiting leaf
As these leaves will wait

Or any eye rolling back
Into its prescription
And the heartache that still rings in the wood
Without any transparent envelope of intention

Only the cover of the sky
The bestiality of the pill

It seems too much to think and see simultaneously

And what, anyway, needs to be there if it's already there?

AN ALTAR OUT OF THE FIELD

On your lips, there it is, inexplicably
Constructed and whole, weathered beyond
Recognition, but still

Ready to wreck the frame, to leave
In flames all of your typos,

Light of the coastline's theory
In thick layers and labors
Of disbelief (or mist as

You'd meant to have it)
What underlines your surface variety—

        The sky may even break
        out of its blank space
        for an hour or two—

Opening up, a kingfisher races through
The pattern, or lack of One—

As slowly they devolve
        Those monks out
        in a far recess of summer,
        playing pinochle—

What it may be to know, out
Of all context, the origin
Of one's lack of context,

The sky still waiting to break
Out of its shell

But that still
Has nothing whatsoever to do

With what this thing is
Supposed to be.

But to be still.

SWILL

Doesn't need to
Beg, to belong, to believe
In either of us.

So forget what I said earlier
About forgiveness, about the basement, salt for anxiety—

Rising steel-toed.
Reel then, not now.

Sky sleeps in the road, doll-fed but still
Deficient, somehow. For a future,

It just needs to fall in with that
Tarmac's murderous glare.

The pill on the grassy knoll
Glows still
Keeps the piece.

DOWN BY THE TOWER

I can co-locate here.
I won't digress, not with these
Metal parts in the desert wind,
Not with a bank of clouds
Stored on film.

A-crawling off
The page, I let the word, the "spider-rack,"
Burrowed fluxulently in the salt
Of its own head, go.

Isaiah Bipolar, in oak and bamboozled,
Felt the room retaining
Its overtly advertent dimensions, and began
To weave the non-sequitur that only
Faith may envelop with her tankers tanked

In a seedy tavern in Tombstone,
Chowed-down, and hung
Like a plastic bag from this twisted
Branch, with Shoes By Imelda.

EATING QUINOA AND SPELT

It is here, inside the lacquer
Of this pill, that dawn will eventually break
And leave the rock to slip away.

Grass still unstrung and damp.
It fills your head with a fitful and picture-perfect sky.
Everything ever-changing but not
In your mind's falling branch.

It is the lure of this moment that is seizing up.
It is that which can be loved.
It is the other become your lover.

A LUSH

The leaves are nearly new.

But as these redolent days
Have begun to lengthen,
You still fall evenly into a
Mere smattering of some
Hypersexual myth.

What matters most, then,
Is something gorgeous,
And very slow.

A god on the ranch. Or one at
The piano in late afternoon.

Getting sleepy?

So am I.

Wallace Stevens falls into the seemingly
Green green seawater:

DAY SLEEPER

It is pointless, yes,
But still possible to raise the dead scope
Out of the living, to wipe away

The dry leaves and phlox
In the last stigmatic flash of a burnt down
Wall of light, it is all or nothing that will

Return, and if at all, much of it
Unchanged, only recoiled for violence, without suspense,

Slurps of booze, filmic illusion, the line
Trimmed in molting lead, delextuals,

Stolen eye now swelling

      Into the detritus of moon
          Over apartment marsh

What was it to arrive with an ease of spirit
In the washing away?

Of things and/or ideas, whatever
               You decide,
Okay, if a climax can bring forth any contrast,
To take a little something

Away from the late sun

A flunky on rented furniture, incensed,
Is ready to crack in the shadow of the foundation
      Still any sense

Can be unmade as easily as you are
Mistakenly taken under

The witness of demarcation
Spliced to fit into popular opinion

Some people have even decided to work harder
To rekindle the already scorched rim

To remain
Highlighted, intact, uttered, impotent for privacy, contracted for festivity

Peripatetic and breaking upon a philandering
Moment for others

Not of the same ilk, not positioned this way, to notice
That the branches are there to rescue the sky

Only the corrugation being recognizable
Apparent above the track

Aimless in July
Head unwound

Summer thunder and your other half
Gone without a glimpse or tremor

524 E. 11TH #9

Never mind. The path will lull you
Into a deep sleep. You don't need
A sound mind here. Forget
The worksheet. Fine example of one

Though it may be, particularly at random. Take
Your recorder out with you and create
A crime to report. Shoot the fine
Specimen as it should be. It shouldn't be all

That hard really. And at the very least
It will get you out of the house, thinking
That you may have a purpose. I know, I know,
That's laughable. But still in the violet

Cynosure you can suit yourself to, the snow
May come down with the fertile promise
Of a nearly new world, overgrown with stinging nettles,
Pierced nipples, green needles, and as far away

From Baghdad as it is from Phoenix. Hey,
Just what the hell is that crimson blotch over there,
Over in the on-going, hovering at the entrance?
All ablaze without end-stops? But the line breaks

Up grace, your façade that leaves nothing out, nothing in.
What was revealed had only left the hint of a line-squall,
And that, as always. Better than can even be imagined,
Unrehearsed, those dogs sleep in their infinitely fine margin.

COLLECTING EVIDENCE

Where is he that counted the towers? (Isaiah 34:18)

As they were thought they were found to be, it was

Unexceptionally unremoved
Then fell in

Okay, now I'm not asking you not to
Wait, okay, I'm not

Out with the plumber who went to prison

I serrate myself with the search ring
As the tower begins to decompose

Activity on the memory card
But it ain't no distortion that'll benefit anyone
I could care about

Anyway, I'm making a copy of this, brother
Just to be on the safe side

Instead, I could be getting on
A plane now
The way I keep thinking about being
And flying to you

How come your double don't bark that way?
I mean bank that way?

More and more
The contributor comes to you

We drain our drinks
As though awash with interest,
Dabbling in the coda,

Layered in the dust of gaping remonstrance,
Dabbled in Dakota

But to devour the moment, even if only momentarily
Embedded in a quasi-professional position,
That's bad for business, which isn't yours in the first place,
Coming through that conventional gate, into all that is good,
Now extending the initial sequence into precedence
Into clinical deceit and cultural vengeance
Into exculpation

But nothing in me provides
For the heater in the mirror

Slowly for the brambles
Case of the sun taken in

FEAR OF NOVELTY

Don't stop to utilize yourself. Carry the lucky
Bamboo into the ash, and into the stream. You

Are already wading peacefully, losing the need
For that stenographic self. Climb the ready shore,

And suppurate. Allow the deciphering. Sand
Is good. Especially wet sand. The coils will

Have flown aimlessly away, and an easy sense
Of presence will be restored, though not on disk.

The incentive never sleeps, making it hard
To imagine the possibility of arriving at two

Separate entrances at once, but that is how
Each moment precedes you, and inhabits you.

It is good for a laugh, even a forced one. As
The questionnaire disintegrates, call upon

Your lover, and begin to appear again. Get down
Upon the wet sand and entwine, ever so sweetly.

This may seem like heaven, and it is without
Speech. You are both inside that bowl of cherries.

THE CRACKHEADS

The rock here beside
The newly framed trees is ready,
Having been handled gently, planted,
And we are in place. We've found
The glass pipe, which will burn
And break. And we are all
In this together. It is obvious
And certain that a strange
Variety of affection will
Descend and ascend within us,
And money will somehow appear.

A stolen debit card and a pin-number
Sent in from the street. Close those
Blinds. And if you cut your lip
On the cracked pipe, you will cut open
A layer of that over-casting sky. See
Beyond it, to the form of your own
Ragged ghost. Let it dance
In the created clearing. Not part
Of the exfoliated field, and in it,
You are all of it. The mouthpiece.

The leaves are turning
Towards you. There is lack
But it isn't epic. The day is quietly
Disappearing, and departing
For other rooms. That's the way
Things are when anything amounts
To a gospel of walled-off reverence.
Because each time I forget the next.
Just an eye that floats off, after all.
It depends upon an arbitrary tone.

There are many things that now seem
Familiar to us, and I suppose that

We should make the effort to believe
That they are real. We need another
8-ball right now. For the next
Few hours. Someone needs to make

the run. Then, in a corner
of the courtyard, the world will take
all of its lines and misquote them.
It's a speculation that attacks itself.
The construction of an almost
Magical virtuosity has caused
A bottle of Stoli to appear beneath
The eye-shadow-blue valium bush.
We down that and need yet
another. It is in this repetition
That I know your second head
Will grow and begin to wobble.
White and hot. Without time,
But stricken by form. How unstruck

Is the line that only sticks. The series
Deliberately begins to sink. It's just
Here to kill off enough shadow
To go on without being canceled.
To taste the charcoal. In the cool
Shallows, I felt like no one else.
I felt like I should be doubling-down.
Someone whose coarse sound
Could cause the whole damn vessel
To submerge. But that's someone else
Now with the wet leaves and the shakes.
The nexus lacks a soft widening
Of the sky, or the news from Afghanistan.
If any thinking occurs, it is only
In the anecdotal fissures that form
Out of a slight horizontal context.
Your mind is in a trench, waiting
On the simple eight, and now there is
Nothing but a conventional outline.

There's no end to anything now.
There's no reason to think there ever was.
The sky has shut down, behind
The drawn shutters. All we have left
Is a little beer for the balancing act.
Throw a net over the nude in the cage.
If only this suffocating space didn't seem
So real, then there would be no point
In hoping that it didn't. To break open.
To leave our self-deception out on the grass
Like the morning dew with the watchdog.

Then the semblance of any structuring
Device would dissolve, leaving only a residue
Of fall color to go on blazing without.
Fate contingent upon abstract strokes
Of the decaying year. The distances
Between us lessening, and the beauty
Of the unknown world coming to
Reinstate all the shady dealings.

We drank something until it was
Nearly dawn, and the new day seemed
Like it had already been cremated
And its ashes placed in a incredibly
Startling jar. Still, it's only the outside.
What was here is gone. But something
Deeply personal is spilling out of each
One of us. I'm starting to crash, and so
Are you. Or have you already?

LATCH/THATCH

Just to get a little slack, and that being
     a few months of free rent, a fractured wing
       before the maintenance begins again; that is
To begin again, at ease, as everything seems
       to have fallen into place:
            rocks, trees, the commingling
          of thought once ruptured into an emptiness of work,
Let's say it has been a pleasant winter, not so
   striating as others, nowhere near
      that city by the Great Lake, and its solid
       body of ice, bungled conversions,
A certain violence one feels to be
     more truthful than oneself,
       the "way" as it will always be tapped.
But I'm leaving now. Time to get out there
   and spread some of that rock around.

THE PRESENT

That which came wrapped up in
Old newspaper, weeds, a frilled lizard
Skin, and the law which must be
Torn open if one is to enter the innermost
Layers of the package, and there to behold
More than a mere mouthful of escape
Clauses, but millions upon millions
Of bootlickers.

BLURB

That that day is going
to be today

remains to be seen.
And not heard. Like children
in a bar. The only one we ever
patronize anymore, because

they've been 86'd from all
the others.

STILT 1

What are you staring at?

Low variable rate.

Twenty minutes left to decide
Come back again unscrewed
In the next twenty.
Pines sweating and metal fingers swaying.

Back to delectation, face against a wall
Of pills. Nice deep pool (old pal)
Fed to viability. Absolute mask
Of the native-born past to tear in half.

I'm twitching beneath the brightest
Moon to appear in decades.

Stepping into 7-11 for cigarettes, narrative
Decay, and there, sleeping on the floor
Is that horribly damaged and demented fool
I'd spoken to in the bar a few hours before. A half-
Eaten sandwich falling out of his hand.

Face against a wall of wild drool.
Nice deep pool (old pal).

An insomniac dabs a little glue
On her pillowcase.

Come back again unscrewed.
Fed to viability. Absolute mask.
She is only one of the many things
I want to be that won't wait.

No wait. The brightest
Moon to appear in decades.
The great moisture fetch
In Wendover, Nevada.

What are you staring at?

I'm just about to break
Even.

STILT 2

It feels better,
Mixed with the formula, wrapped up for ritual space,
Not to me, but for you,

Watch the leaves, unequal lighting, any want
You choose, watch them fall and forget
Your proposal,

Seaweed/Rental Agency,

It's poverty, naturally, Mr. Blacklawn
That sends you
To the gun show,
And yes, it's yours, it's to be
In a loophole,

Ascendent/Undifferentiated,
Redrawn like an election line,

The utter incongruity of reliability at the center,
The inarticulate skewer without clear progression
Towards the palatial meat, that without averted bone

And tantalizing suet in the cornices:

Violate the rock: Honey, manifest dyslexia

Lead sun on the collar indoing stresses

O pony-head: Bite the Babylon ::: Fixed up and on
O nauticals without glass

       Flank steak
       Dawn its ear

Sky drags back and swallows
Sun under water

Head seal
Sump

STILT 3

And someone had tossed

   A dildo
      Out onto the tracks

      Of the El   And all around it   It was just
   As it was   It was just as it is
          After all

      It was just   A half-hit brother

And it looked like   A black dildo

          All around it

            There was something   Sleazeminola

That was a part   Of everything else

       The airbag deploying   All around it

    Box-cutters being boxed   Infirmities
Being bound

   To the big old trees   Had twaddled

Off into the warmth

      Of theory   The huge

           Vacated lot   The skyline

Disintegrated   And the new city

      Anchored to starlessness   O the endless
Swill

STILT 4

As you were
Saying: Everything is
        So Freaking precious and I
      Mean it: God moon and Vagrancy
          Made routine as

                               As promised

                            fate
Preordained: Its identity blotted out: Twine again   veil
                            Heroic contact

As you were saying: Is everything
      But small change depocketed on

                 The rictus sea   The child slept on
      Through the Viennese sunset   Drooled on
The document on the floor   Came back with impetigo

        Some drunks
        Chuckled
            Others called their sponsors

         Left it
    To the moon

They thought the document was too real

But still
There has to be   Some pleasure
                   In hanging
      On to

    This artificial
Lighting

STILT 5

But still

There has to be
    Some chromatic dragonfly

  Gone   A-Field

Without artificial flavoring

                Wearing the way and away
            Everything and anything
You can get
    Your hands on   The wolves in Central Park

    Depocketing your neighbor   For instance: Here

At 5000 feet the rain

                Manzanita   fall in with
                              the wine-dark
    Now crystallizing   snow   branch
                  Smack   that prevaricates

At 5000 feet in a flurry now

        Straggling back to further

      Lies all laid   :Pull the blinds

        Forbearance and deferment
      Require different forms

STILT 6

Leaping the turnstiles

      So easily and
        Now what?

Now that it seems

          Italicized into myriad
Shadow
           To be in   embedded

So you have nothing to worry about

But still there has to be   Hey you   With the morning high

           Fill the stream and mine

          With that dragonfly wine that leaps
       The ruinous turn-
Stile

But no   forget that   all of it   never mind

You still wouldn't be
       There would you?

STILT 69

Parts to steal, slipped off
The scenic exaggeration, so, love
Let's go and get it done.

       Get tiled and tilted,

       Get covered in these leaves,
       The metallic blue butterflies.

Note how we are
Stretched along a trick shore, and at ease,

      Cradling a small deer in our arms

The flares in the west
Going up—   Fixed up and over again, over
           Again, at random
           In the paradise

Of that presence,
This present, so, love
Now you are here, so

Relinquish it
As it relishes you.

STILT 7

Or two tumblers full
Of Sandy Brown holding a tray
Of terrific-looking sushi
At Christopher Sunset.

I woke up in it, at it
Slumping into its shrug of dope
And cementing Kansas. Shaggy,
We've quaffed enough of holy cunted
Pearl for Christopher Sunset
To feel slightly reassured,
Even ready to run off

A few copies. Copies of the gleam
On that tongue. Rose in the bed.

STILT 8

But still there has to be   Each evening The geese flying in formation
From the artificial lake to the golf course at sundown   Sunset that is
Tearing off an orange peel and scattering the rind   A sunset so beautiful
And mandarin but not without a suggestion of sedition   And contrails
Both military and commercial   Cutting across this   Cocktail made
To fall tonight like a paperweight And other parts of the sky still holding
To magenta rose and the empurpled tail You know You're one of them
Held together by broken layers that do your speaking for you   Down
In the park with curry powder corn cobs a choked cigar and a moment
To make   Someone twinge and cut the goat's neck with a quickening
Squeal   Go down to the county clerk with a little slipper full of fresh
Blood It's best   To drink at dawn, out on the pier if possible, out of
Your paper bag, out out

Damn silicon muses   Long after the sun has burnt down But first, twist me
Into your irregular trees, until the sparrows are placed in the vinaigrette,
And the sunflowers on the yoga mat And on this flattened rock let
There be an all-maddening music to procure the rack with utmost care
A new face for the sozzled
Along the lines of these bark beetles
That destroyed all of my pines in one summer-long binge
You could say it was a dehortation of sorts, a vehement urging if you will, to
Take down the ventilators at once, to risk it all on one hand, and to freak

In the sawtooth of the delivery, a filthy bird dying in the plastic six-pack
Connector at the dumpster right now, someone is drunk It's all yours Isn't it
Time to stop thinking   That's why I came here   Dogs getting wet
That's the little pond for the city run-off   I came out here early
To drop   It's all my valium in the grass and another doctor to be lied to
To drop   God I'm getting itchy now here in the gesture, and wet legs on
Display   And I know   you're gonna have a hard time swallowing this   But
Aspirin Zyprexa Beer & Mashed Potatoes ain't so bad together Twist
In the snout
Start over is all I
Ever pour into the heater

Censoring the sky   It's the way of the park to bend   Just as you thought
You could stand up   Mistake the mis-take of yourself as another
Not the fatted calf   Oh I'm just taking out the garbage   Help me before
These diagonals take over   Make these keys light   Light up another
Though the inflexibility is real   It is now that memory rolls over
The painted rocks   Like us the living water   Sublacustrine

STILT 8 ½

Outside of Inner Ovenbird   licks up
    Lives   all lies   in the animal
  Advanced in anti-coalescence   the animal will outer What's
Her name? Our Lady of the Diagnostic Flame
        Will only array   with the ingrate
    Sun down downing the whole
        Son already downed   Jenny and I
Sleep in   Out here?   Before crossing over
  To Outer Inska   with relevants
    Peering out   from the opening
Of the colossal   structure
    That bears down   On
Ward   Wired under
  World

REVOLUTION #9

Up all night   gone in
Go in   Stick the dirty quarter
In your mouth   I've been here before   winter-color and sink-dome
I fall in   snipe the succulent   bite
                        Identical pariah has it   What fabric?
    Kept half-time.   Course in you the creepy.   Gone now
Smooth.   Stick the quarter
In my mouth again.   Going in for what?   Canned
  In the first   control.   Back in.   You know this.   Give they group?
Gone   middle tongue   stuck in moon   the mannequin is most
Moist   first thing remote   cut and remove   them   head and limb are
Not here   to say it is   Crank-yoko is
What is going on   to be known   all snipe on   glistened
We feel known   if only in the knowing   that glam   rain over railway
    It came down   to touch   in limitless
            Glass strangers   quote called tongue-is   too red with bark
Sleeps on good board
Quarter   stick it in my mouth   dirty summer   day all diatribe   windowpane
Strange soaking   land and   must land   easy for you   ever   at last
    That in being   notes leaves in cars   piercing re: to j   almond butter
There is not going to be one is there?   Coke-yoko.   Leaves left
Somewhere in that   descry   imagine it all   mad ailanthus   broken
    Sleepy summer well   we went down   So
            It is all a pierce   but when down came back up
All one good as another   But then
A card to carry bombs   it's called   they say it   is called   it is   repetition
No one could   hold out   holed-in   ripe orange   bark sleeping not well
        Something rattles   moon sticks to mock   we're just not
The same   it does seem to open   itself
Ever so slightly   But if you're not
Really ready   the unimaginable it   I mean I can't take off
These years   when no one is treatable   take the presentability   these then
All always screening   wherefrom outlet   No I will not   blot   because
There isn't any more   sprawl   it can't   handle
Yours   in the past   life literally without
Track   not if he has a lot   But I said

All my relatives are megalomaniacs   clear outlet   where is
The number   god save the timber   the tumbler   can't read paycheck   can't
Figurate   the best and brightest   appearance harasses   everyone see   seams
Junk too   admitted   herein trailhead got the rubber boots here comes here is
Something   living   wants to go back   there again   then again   de-junk Jah
And John in 99999

STILT 9

Though now again too late   to repair the twisted
In explication   Though now again   the frame steadies   an arm hangs
Down   into the diminishing utterance   the measly digression   the cruelty
Vectors   A birth unlikened to belief   pressed into the power station
Pacified   Only the urge to plunge   Onto the projection   into open space
But it isn't at all   It calls up definition   The full bottle that is best
For nothing but   Being still   Still at some distant point   the open vial
The purely astonishing moment   of interaction   in the same water
The glue   the elasticity   the polish already drying on tomorrow
As it calls up   wine   olives a reddening sky   stilts   wine   face-paint
A pill to bait the ghost   pill in the sun   no need to wait
Until you may become   as fake as you are intentional   visible
To the lovers   sea-salt   rimming the margaritas   say it is   a rippling
Dawn down under   say it is   having it both ways   dubbed
The lapse   rush expands   but not to erase   not here anyway   not
For something so close   directed towards you   the sign
Finding its hole   awash   bright and away   and the state still
Cut off at the ears   a contraption   that waits wantingly without
Hot white   goats available for boilerplate   searing zone
In the overlay   the pederant tube   hanggliders fill out the left
No stable edge   but draw together   and divert the occasion   it is
Your self-guided tour   there on the cover   and now the early   softening
Of the light   sifts the grove   now once again   my love
The evening stills   for a moment
There is the moon

STILT 10

If the pressure was taken out   Leaving you to be   God   Easy and formless
A fall as metallic blue   As the butterfly's preternatural exception
No sense   Of self-criticizing fracture   Other genres   Hence a theory held
In a very soft drink   A doberman is whining for a bit of that bagel   Immersion
In sound   In cruelty   Grace always arbitrary   Still it shifts
Will always leave Its stain Upon the stranded In sleep's neutrality But how
Is one to arrive   Casual and late   In what is being?   In what won't seek
To reappear in magnification?   The dog's ears cropped   The tail cut

Satan is still Incomplete A collapsible sky Caught up in transaction Factoried
At birth   Chrome eye   Always part faith and part germ on the grid   Daybreak
Draws back   From a lit wire to a living assortment of overtly-prismatic dreams
Day untied   Take the answer out of the question   Pull out the wanted mood
Put it on public notice Paint yourself a disciple Make the exchange with the devil
Roses now in the rear-view mirror   Bite down hard   Eat the last   Fat margin
Born of the branches   But stay out of this   Theme-park   Reading is for sadists
Mainly swept into the corner   By self-same   Nomadic saliences   Left untouched
By interpretation Or temporal coordinates Only a flask-full Of open-ended-ness
Of the world   Destroyed by familiarity   Divided
Any other   Inaccessible

STILT 11

The carafe empty, and now to clay   bamboo scaffolding
My bones empty, and now to documentation   knife eases
The moon empty, and now to Blake   fennel well-defined, but
  In which frame

The leaves to eat, and now to blur
The edges   Such a lingering autumn   Yellow November in mid-
  Construction   All becoming wet and ready

  To fall
Away, and now to being unsaid   willow grove
Finger up your ass   3-dimensional state   One comes
          Logistically, and now to unfolding   process process   torn absolute

Will not defamiliarize, and now to convention
Some tablets reserved   Polyglots gone mad, and now to raw jellyfish, so blue
  Beneath the singular

Evening awaited, and now to be withheld   roses on fire   wracked pulse
Put your portrait on anyway,
  And now to inevitably retrace the rain Apollinaire refracted, go on

Get out
Get caught in the brambles, and now to bleed   Opening still
  Shines but sinks deeper   it just wants more
Wine, nothing that tapers off, and will

Not download pastorality, and now to exhale
  Consistent though double
  And now to the thorax   supra-human sunglasses

Footing unstable, and you the sifted
Violence of untold millennia, and to remote the remote   steel cups
  And the leaking cartridge

STILT 12

Waking up to wine and apple sausage
                        The sky seemed to break
            Out of the shelter of its rosy fingers   groveling over the genre of native ground
                    The last face carried   how the briefcase forced a flickering
                Away   This was not the time
                                To tremble into contrast   alienation mapped out
Also eggs red potatoes bourbon
                            Nothing could make it last   soaking weeds
                            Cocaine heart   sense of adventure
            Humanity lost   though still unremoved   life as event   the ice
Looked somewhat like ganglia   where it had begun to melt   face unfaced
        Well face it anyway   Stars being snuffed   out of your way of knowing
Coming out   at the joints
                    Even here you couldn't be   served   past into lead
                                                Paint
        In the dim light a communal trace   it's that groveling
                                        Again in the layers
                    The tracks   in the mud   on the wrist   Hinge
To disarticulation   doubling down   to drink freely in the doubling dawn
            Still   we were expected   to be in the blaze   poured out Fuck me
        In the missing   face   paint   weed   In that wild yet   cased
        Valley floor   lately   served   Soaking in it   yet still   wildly
Unface me   no contrast for native ground but absolutely walled-off and soaked
    Into the uncontainable abstraction   that which the alien might feel
        Wholly in the gap   taken up from what tears down   down in want Fuck me
Contingency   to fill in   the face   What other? Viewpoint vaporized? This
        Can only   come apart indefinitely   since its sanction is internal   Check
The message board
Taste the equilibrium being restored
This thing can't reface me   but now the surface sticks and affirms
I want to give something to Sandrine Bonnaire   mine own French actress

NEW TO THE AREA

Exhale and come into the Cobra. The shades in your mind
Are conventional, the torrential downpour of a sky
Being downloaded. You've been watching it from the porch.
They're modeling in mother-of-pearl, coincidently.

Do not begin to obsess. At least, not quite yet. Take this,
Take that, and then find your way back. The reader "eats"
But only to externalize emotions otherwise unsteadying.
Premeditation cannot lead to the pastoral, not with real turf.

But it's getting ahead of itself now. The security
Of the fictitious is only that. A cerulean nurse-goddess.

No, not of this place. Not ready for a cosmology
Of any kind. That appearance of self-awareness. To use
Oneself as an extra-literary source. To become
Recognizable in any manner or degree of differentiation.

This is what it had in mind. This gave a purpose
To an ironic ideology. It is now to be born upon that branch.

CHARGES

Being still   (though we've been gone)
  (long enough)   and on the whole
Away   from the pursuit   (of coming into it)
I am ready   (it still went back)   to pull
The stops   out of this   externality   (though wholly dependent
    upon that moisture)   And hasn't it become
Too easy to notice   that which isn't

Reeling off   (sporadic in a hint)   outside the entrance
Face to face   (but without dimension)   at Crystal Corner
  (A starving Chihuahua)   (indiscriminately obscene)
That bar   turned   (towards the one
    returning)   (always leaning)   into the meat
By the falls   (always leaning primally)   (Go ahead: Eat it!)

A hole   (gaping)   in the setting   Idiomatically mixed
Were our drinks   (leafing out)   as was the kiosk

GETTING CHAINY

I know what needs to be done now.
I'm going to walk, as though in
   slow-motion, across the street and spit on those
People's cat. Then I'll return
   for the "divining" rod, as the benevolent chill
   seeks me out, and fills me with that sheer indifference
That emanates from the deep core
Of some pathetic internal
      conflict. What? No, not mine you idiot. It means
That your medication is working the way
That it's supposed to,
         and bending out the indicators
That were lent to lead you on.

Get out, please.

Fetch my dogs some ice-water.
   With slices of lemon, if that's not
Asking too much of you, you miserable
   pedant. You know what it is now, don't you? It's time
To relinquish the "time-line," the serial
Modifiers, 2003 UB 313, that photo-tropic
   behavior which you rush
Into after a swig of Telepathic Order. Because, you see, for me
There is always the certainty
   of the Circle Tour from Big Bone Lick
To Rabbit Hash to Sugartit and back again
To Bone.

BACKWARDS

You know what it can be like.
There in the car. Waiting so

Damn tediously for that is so. An exploitation
Of the sign system this. May be

Life. Nothing solves.
It salivates. Then showers

Alone. Light lifting rock.
Wet grass now unstrung.

Torn to birding. Landing upright?
Fallen branch our serenade.

A clue? Some glue?
That's why not. I won't

Wake up. Even in the dark to a deer.
Made arbitrary. No key. Go.

DEAD HORSE POINT

But if it was only going to call us out
This far, we figured it would have been
Best to have just junked the whole
Junket altogether, let someone else
Take the heat, which was
Getting sort of intense, more than a mere
Contrivance, which is what
We had been
Seeking, for as long as we could
Remember, come to think of it, all along.

BEFORE DAYBREAK

No moisturized
Sordid mess of meaning has yet
To be meant

To be driven through
Some previous sketch

It being one that one
Could break open
Gently to the juice if chosen

But time now for X
Is running short

The spread of a seemingly
Unfiltered non-entity
Has begun to take on shadows
Has already taken itself back

HOTEL HALLIBURTON

I can't remember which ones I forgot
To use. The wicked slope being shaped
By what happened while I was out.
I went back to the bar, but now with paint
On my shoes and socks, unaware that I had
Returned, so to speak. Miss me?

You were over in the park, downing
Your cheap shots in the dark, fabricating
History, releasing the fatigued from questioning
What had already been answered for them,
Inadequately of course, the close stills,
A dose of calculated inaccuracy in your dead

Reckoning, just as a blast
Of democratic dawn lights up
The deep
Middle of the night.

FROZEN EMBLEM

On each corner, voices that
   Backed up the chain-saw, ordered
Sinister tables to be set up
   To mark the chewing
Of the tablet. O perdition,
   And respiration, very low.
There, then, the long projection
   Of the chosen syllable
   Sent the haughty wreathings
   Blindly into forgotten space.
The scattering of the multitude
   Always leaves its stain.
That which, if noticed, will
   Trace your fitful movement
   Across the margins
   Of its sky. Not yours alone.

26 LINES

It was said in such murderous glare
That is was very difficult to understand.
I tried, but I still couldn't resist the urge
To smash something over your head.
It was, I figured, merely the burnt hand
Of that blinding sky coming unhinged

To its reckless abandon; its alone, not mine
And not yours, not Thoreau's, not even now
In and of itself. It doesn't make any sense,
I know, but it's now yours to handle, fondle even,
As is. If and when there is an as is, as you
Have had your target of opportunity, but now

Are falling endlessly through the metal rupture
With ice forming on your fingernails and idiosyncratic
Fiber, all of which has been blown away mercilessly
In the fierce wind of supercilious contraction, and
Those that have never fully become luminous
With contradiction. It is something that will not

Release a flea, the ancient box, the backseat
Of the car that blended you, the drift of the oiled
Drum carrying the small pond away, the devils in
The brilliant leaves that have barely been dreamt up
Or imagined before are now filling it all out,
Are filling up your mouth, leaving your wild eye

Safe and satisfied, though still floating towards that
Which it has always wanted, adjuration, the rain.

IT ALREADY KNOWS YOU

They shouldn't show up too soon.
Not before all probability of formal
Engagement with the wild has begun
To fade. And there is the room full
Of sardine tins to be dealt with as well.
They will not be cut as cleanly as the coming
Personalities in their pastel robes.
But there's no telling what this endlessly
Layered weather will cause anyone
To be forced to face. To scarf down, but
Only real bugs have sucking mouth-parts.

Affect has evolved into compliant seasons.
It leaves the powder-blue glue-sniffing
Front revolving like the door it is. There
Is plenty more to be said about this, but
It needs a silk knot to sense its arrival.
If there is going to be change, it can't
Be too specific about its motives, but
It does need to involve a clearly
Noticeable plethora of lacerations.
And though the wine is cheap, I think
You'll be willing to drink it anyway,
As you don't really have much choice.
The real process is continually missing.
It can't seem to locate its coordinates.
It is only the leaves falling, filling in
The fountain of random mayhem.

Nothing here can fathom what is meant.
The roots are suspended above the ground,
Dangling in the shallow air. So it is simply and always passing,
But through it passes so much, even that which you didn't
Have to come to care about. Late at night, holding a revolver
In one hand, and some morsel in the other, not part of the present,

Through which a laugh comes off the glass, the glass you drank from,
Blindfolded, thinking on and outward while the transaction was being
Made, made to be in a private mode, you sought any opening, the coming
Unstrapped, shanked off the bone, chewing the content not merely contradiction,
The same channel is always on, willing to be endured, muted, or enjoyed

With a mouth full of dust, a head full of ecstasy to feel each other out
Casually, without a sound, enveloping all there is to be had
In chemical serenity, down to it in off-being, may the elements be
Spared a recklessness of mixed genres, genes misconstrued in the silhouette,
The ventriloquy of the field came to be what it wouldn't be called, but then
We're always dealing with amateurs, leaving the porch light on all night,
The vector miscalculated, and a crash course in troubled weeping, the same
Old behavior was being described, trading in your broken tools for drinks,

Still, it wasn't enough to let you sleep, to go into the flare of a severality
Of dream, though it smolders all around you in wayward passions, in the stark
Beauty of a simple moonrise, verdure, maybe some valium and violet sleaze,
Virginia Plain, but the cut that will mark you out still seems to be missing,

The late call in the evening, everything that couldn't get done, it sends you
Northbound on Southport, fluctuating again, but you're not alone now, are you?
Do you remain stubbornly detached from the hereafter, assuming there is such
A ludicrous realm to calm your nerves? Why haven't you given away all that

You saved for? Listen closely and you'll know that there's no one that you are
Listening to. You don't put one word after another. You put them inside each
Other. Rattle that jar, and mix it up behind the blue dolphins on your
Shower curtain. That will leave you with nothing left to revise, and so it is.

PLAGIARIZE IT

I didn't want to believe you were a Martian
But you left me no choice. I drank a lot of beer.
I thought about burying you up to the neck and
About how little is left that can actually be controlled.

The insert.
The mind itself alone was not
Alone itself in any of this mess.
All pedantry of the interior apocalypse.

    Upon thy knees
    Thou knowest best
    The bounty
    Of thy beautiful 12-pack

        The loosening thread is that which
        Brings your prototype closer   O

THE SEALING EYE

Early in the day, as the code carries its cargo in,
Everything beginning to slowly bend into shape
Off the rekindled brunt of your brain,
      Forces without gin settling into place,
While a few seem perspicacious to a degree in regard to
  The lemons that the personal-injury lawyer
    Is about to slice, to serrate the splendor
 Of an easy case she's about to pocket, the slot-machines
Will be there when you want to use them with a straw
  In your mouth, steady now and in control
       So that nothing
  Even remotely surreal may spill-
Over, affect the spin, find something pointless
  And figure that it matters, a monstrous silhouette hovering
        Over the reclamation
    Project of your would-be redeemers, just
     Remember that allowing things to work backwards will
Allow them to work out in your favor, sometimes,
    Although the rim is burning and taking down small towns,
Anything can be re-read backwards in the hope of making it
  One's own, but you should know by now
     That you are always its, for Christ's sake
   Already, with your own gin, to contemplate
      In private, stretched out in the circular
   Road, un-alone, with the everlasting suspicion
     That you were always someone else
   Than you thought you were, no surreptitious self-regard
To be handled with a gunsmith's ex-girlfriend, no extenuating
  The circumstances, the land barren far beyond a figure
    Of speech, wasted miles upon miles before you, it gives
Only that parched stare in return, nearly tilted and almost turning
     A strange inversion inside you, as it has
   Grown used to contrivance, a primitive mode
Of coercion carried in the dust-storm that pulls
    You over to the roadside, and leaves you

With the impression that you are in fact the same mannerist
Depiction that you always thought you were,
Veins drained to the circumstance, passions habitual
But not really so harmful, to anyone including yourself,
There is no karma, get over it, life in all its materiality
Spills forth, lips to the soil, a tooth embedded in a rock,
Infidelities light up the approaching night,
Which is where you've always wanted to live, to listen
Closely to the dimensions of your personality out
For the evening in cellophane, rolling sevens
Like a plagiarizing angel, or devil, or both, the reverberation
Of a booklet's description of a creature from far out of space,
The invested systematically calling in, in sloppy hexameter,
Eventually letting go and leaving everything out, including
A chord of recognition, just your club-face
Fixed in a flash, that punishing chance
For transfer into pointlessness, to walk past
The cream counter, the copies of friends, the clangor
Of the overly cooked, but always still
To be and now to be still beneath a pine tree, the sun
Getting cranked up—

NUMEN ANAESTHETIZED

But when it really came down to it
No one had noticed or cared

I had been drinking
A simple glass of milk for the public's benefit

When we saw the Western Tanager in Zion
Near the Great White Throne

But it kept me from wanting to eat

To match my idiotic posture
To yours and to desingularize

To roll the blood orange down
The granite slope that is used here

To find yourself a title without
Smoking any dope or detritus

To wear out the simple wet platform

Going down on the ghouls at 7 a.m.
With a stringent cancellation policy

And drinks served only next
To the dartboard from a bucket of fish

Spines and beryl tablets on the soft-shell
Have what you want but then you gotta

Leave the discharge instructions behind

For the benefit of the staff
Whose relic of a motive it is to
Dismantle the boundaries of time

Hobbling down the stone staircase
Carrying the poison of seditious doctrines
Farther even than it shall seem
To their own eyes so wily and crafty

Every day bringing supernatural ritual to ordinary space
That being indirect
That being due to the vicissitudes
The tails being arbitrary enough but

The non-sequitur not being
Real enough in that being
Not enough of the numinous

Eumenidesian in the mix
To make all of this touch seem so real so
The karaoke bar is bound to
Bring it all back to us

But who knows who might still audition with blind ambition

To be still and willing to go out
To the old Rambler
To inhale some ancient gas

And come back the same
Only with an eyeball slightly out of place
An infusion of spirits being called for and shook out

But as usual I was out somewhere
Rubbing myself with roots and grasses

That's it that's all that's that that's the glaze still drying

THE LONG WAY AROUND

No, wait. That's not all. There's more, and plenty of it. But it's not
Something entirely replicable as it gets rolled. Besides, mistakes are made
All the time. In picking out shoes or placing someone on death row,
Perhaps on the same day. If you could find yourself on the cover
Of a botanical journal, could you release yourself from the bitter cold
Of calculation? And could it be true for everyone that you've ever
Given the slightest thought to? Take this, for instance, that the green

Instant is insistent and has matched itself to your flattering sense
Of finding yourself once removed from all of those pale and tedious
Obligations you have to meet, and that the various tracks of observation
Were yours now for the choosing, a bewildering iridescent sky now meshed
Upon the canal zone, where love is spilled in hidden rose petals, far away
From the over-articulated security of the offices by the Falls, but not
The fall of one single red leaf in October that wears us out, and sends
Us into the beautiful clarity of oblivion. The trees may seem to carry
A coated, ambiguous cast, but they do not seem arbitrary. I finally got out

Of the overstuffed party in the ordinary apartment, and became unglued.
The moon was low in the eastern sky, and I imagined the taste of a French
Actress as I turned in that direction. Mad ailanthus tears up the deliberate
Evening that has fallen but has not forgotten to mock itself, with stars and the
Mystery of its ever-present magnetism that may be a form of revenge. There
Are just too many damn people moving around and looking comfortable, even
Amidst the collateral damage. There is a burnishing, a clusterfuck glowing

In one corner. Will it cancel you out if you stop to consider it? Brittle leaves
Being described in that. Is there something the same in the two that should
Cause you to care, the next quote being placed in the mouth of a surly park
Ranger, and some areas of the surrounding imprecision being more ready
To be easily enjoyed? I started to snooze on the fifteenth green of the nearby
Golf course, but only very briefly as it left me feeling even more contained
Than I had been before I left. The field was taking on the quality of iron,

Or a storage facility for grass and weeds. It had that call of an arrival about it.
That which would not be willing to leave you with the possibility of getting

Out, or getting enough. Is it because you've never been able to find a theme
To let the table-top revolve on? Leaving it to rot out in the rain, the fetish
Of a cherished uncertainty. Note that it has been able to rattle you a bit, that
It is borrowing your time and money. Interrupting you in bars and daytrips
To some adobe ruins, talking all the time, always starting to whisper at dawn.
Whatever it is that is coming, it is coming to be more unknown than it had been.
Back in the days when the skies were seamless, or at least there was a lack

Of rote formation to be kept engaged. The jet fighters rarely flew over these hills,
The tongue-piercings, the tangelos in the supermarket, the broken promises, all
The fascination one might be able to feel, with the calm that was. Everything that
Goes into continuing after you're finished. The whole pine-a-hum, wall-eyed, in
The wedge of willing away, in the shot of tequila that smudges something out
For the time being. Her weird gaze rusting on the moment as though it were
Repeating itself. More than a long scratch from a bleeding tree, a transgression was
What was being called for, almost anything would do, to fill in for the sun's insistence
On bringing into view an entire spread of substances meant to render the bringing
On of the being inedible. Four continuous nights of bombing. In it, the bottle
That is brought to your lips seems sinister and bitter. Good for nothing but being
Still, being unable to refuse. Being in anything that can't be finished off. Being

A hanging chad. To believe in coming off without leaving a trace. Nothing left
To medicate in the damped-out zones of missed recognition. To burn down
The buildings in the dead of winter, a full moon on a Saturday night. The colors,
As they began to machinate, reminded you of the dollars spilt into the stream,
Now gone dry. You'd wanted to slip into the gnarly slot-canyon as our dirty
Chairs began to play upon their heads. Blown out into a barren field, the wreck
Of the sun died again, back into rehearsal and twisted branches, dyed. Outside
Its sign, it finds its hole still smoldering after two months, but that's another
Story, isn't it? Are you bound into a position that cannot translate you? May
Something strange be asked of us each temperate day, and break the frame?

Do you still want it to be the same way we always fell for one another, or there
At the bank in the rising unfamiliar light of dawn? The way is falling, and the
Water is failing. Cut the circuits, and leave the spaces on the forms blank. It
Quickly gets to the point where you can't stand being wasted, but there's no
Point in being not. Knot ready. A slur in the speech, a lament for the salivating,
Lachrymose and splintering land off the old ramshackle sky of disintegrating
Subdivided lawns. Wild horses in the clearing stretch the deception. The tame

Pheasants were nevertheless released and shot. This is not a tie-dyed light, this
Has no desire to be glossed-over, this fat bastard represents you. Rent-free. Get
Mirrored-up in your exploitation, whatever that might mean. That not-exactly

Best and brightest look wherever you go, perhaps traipsing along photogenically.
After that it's just one false step after another that leads you into the waiting
Arms of your sponsor, martens above the railroad ties. The student-band splits
A box of crawfish, rotating inside of the rupture, the rapture. That was easy,

That was near a stand of trees that rattled out of the mineral rush, a fresh eel
Feeling its way down your throat. The rare dove is lost in the schizoid sky. She
Said a flag had been pinned to her tongue, a naked revolver in the glass trees.
The sight of the magnolias there was freakish, but, still, you can drink that if
You really want to, and you can put a torch up to the past, put a pen-name on it,
Turn in space complacently yet doubled-up and drawing a pair of killing fives.

LEAVING

Now going away, is being
Given away? A way that is not

Customarily delineated from
The opening of its own

Fissure. Can one glide through
The moment without giving way

To that reductive scratch? Am I thought
Out now, ready to be merciful and free?

I've just stumbled upon this track, but I think it is
Where I need to stay for a while, and rest.

ALWAYS ALWAYS LAND

A little more, but that's all.
Well, okay, a little more, but really,
I gotta mean it this time. Just until
I can taste the snow and mint
On my tongue. After all, I had
A tooth yanked out this morning.

Well, okay, another. Before the flame-green
Jet of propulsion is apparent, in private ways,
Almost unimaginable, the bare branches
Neither sick nor religious, like the birds
Of the rich, and nothing sinister begins
To swing above the wolving brainwork.

Well, then, I wouldn't mind starting over again
And again and again and again.

Even if it's only as early in the day
As you'd figured it was, and nothing
Is about to crush the horizon, or be
Given back, go ahead and have a little more
If you really want it, here at the Shut-Ins
State Park in Missouri, with Jenny. Because

The things you are about to name always
Give way to a gradual dissolving anyway.
La flor la musica grande, the celestial dew.
It's still now though, beneath the obliterant
Whisper and the lovers' now falling sky.
This will never be a minefield, we pray, but
A mere outcropping of rock, a few trees, and
The absolute emptiness of our minds.

Fence Books is an extension of *Fence,* a biannual journal of poetry, fiction, art, and criticism that has a mission to redefine the terms of accessibility by publishing challenging writing distinguished by idiosyncrasy and intelligence rather than by allegiance with camps, schools, or cliques. It is part of our press's mission to support writers who might otherwise have difficulty being recognized because their work doesn't answer to either the mainstream or to recognizable modes of experimentation.

The Motherwell Prize (formerly the Alberta Prize) is an annual series that offers publication of a first or second book of poems by a woman, as well as a one thousand dollar cash prize.

Our second prize series is the Fence Modern Poets Series. This contest is open to poets of any gender and at any stage of career, and offers a one thousand dollar cash prize in addition to book publication.

For more information about either prize, visit www.fenceportal.org, or send an SASE to: Fence Books/[Name of Prize], New Library 320, University at Albany, 1400 Washington Avenue, Albany, NY, 12222.

For more about *Fence,* visit www.fenceportal.org.

Fence Books

THE MOTHERWELL PRIZE

Aim Straight at the Fountain and Press Vaporize   Elizabeth Marie Young
Unspoiled Air   Kaisa Ullsvik Miller

THE ALBERTA PRIZE

The Cow   Ariana Reines
Practice, Restraint   Laura Sims
A Magic Book   Sasha Steensen
Sky Girl   Rosemary Griggs
The Real Moon of Poetry and Other Poems   Tina Brown Celona
Zirconia   Chelsey Minnis

FENCE MODERN POETS SERIES

Star in the Eye   James Shea
Structure of the Embryonic Rat Brain   Christopher Janke
The Stupefying Flashbulbs   Daniel Brenner
Povel   Geraldine Kim
The Opening Question   Prageeta Sharma
Apprehend   Elizabeth Robinson
The Red Bird   Joyelle McSweeney

NATIONAL POETRY SERIES

Collapsible Poetics Theater   Rodrigo Toscano

ANTHOLOGIES & CRITICAL WORKS

*Not for Mothers Only: Contemporary Poets on Child-Getting &
Child-Rearing*   Catherine Wagner & Rebecca Wolff, editors

POETRY

The Method	Sasha Steensen
The Orphan & Its Relations	Elizabeth Robinson
Site Acquisition	Brian Young
Rogue Hemlocks	Carl Martin
19 Names for Our Band	Jibade Khalil Huffman
Infamous Landscapes	Prageeta Sharma
Bad Bad	Chelsey Minnis
Snip Snip!	Tina Brown Celona
Yes, Master	Michael Earl Craig
Swallows	Martin Corless-Smith
Folding Ruler Star	Aaron Kunin
The Commandrine & Other Poems	Joyelle McSweeney
Macular Hole	Catherine Wagner
Nota	Martin Corless-Smith
Father of Noise	Anthony McCann
Can You Relax in My House	Michael Earl Craig
Miss America	Catherine Wagner

FICTION

Flet: A Novel	Joyelle McSweeney
The Mandarin	Aaron Kunin